"Trust Funds Unveiled: How Regular People Can Secure Their Financial Future"

Introduction:

- Explain the purpose of the book: to provide a comprehensive guide on setting up and leveraging trust funds for financial security and growth

The purpose of the book, "Trust Funds Unveiled: How Regular People Can Secure Their Financial Future" is to provide a comprehensive guide that empowers regular individuals to set up and leverage trust funds for financial security and growth.

Trust funds are often associated with the wealthy, but this book aims to demystify trust funds and show that they can be a valuable tool for anyone seeking financial stability and success. The book will break down the complexities of trust funds into simple, jargon-free language, making it accessible to readers with varying levels of financial knowledge.

By offering step-by-step instructions, practical tips, and real-life examples, the book will guide readers through the process of establishing trust funds that align with their goals and circumstances. It will cover various types of trust funds and help readers choose the most suitable structure to meet their needs.

The book will also highlight the benefits of trust funds, such as asset protection, tax advantages, and the ability to provide financial security for loved ones. It will provide strategies for minimizing risk, maximizing investment returns, and adapting trust funds to changing life circumstances.

Additionally, the book will explore the power of trust funds in leaving a lasting legacy through charitable giving, encouraging readers to consider philanthropy as part of their financial planning.

Overall, the purpose of the book is to empower regular individuals with the knowledge and tools they need to unlock the power of trust funds and achieve financial security and growth in their everyday lives.

Chapter 1: Decoding Trust Funds: Demystifying the Basics

- Define trust funds in clear, jargon-free language for regular individuals

Trust funds are a powerful financial tool that regular individuals can use to protect and grow their wealth, provide for their loved ones, and plan for the future. In simple terms, a trust fund is a legal arrangement where one person, known as the "trustee," holds and manages assets on behalf of another person or group of people, known as the "beneficiaries."

The trustee has a legal obligation to manage the assets in the trust fund according to the instructions laid out in a document called the "trust agreement." This agreement specifies how the assets are to be used, distributed, and invested.

Trust funds offer several benefits. They can provide asset protection by keeping the assets separate from personal ownership, making it more difficult for creditors or legal judgments to access them. Trust funds can also minimize taxes by taking advantage of certain tax strategies and allowances.

Trust funds can be used for various purposes, such as providing for the financial needs of children, grandchildren, or other loved ones, ensuring their education, healthcare, and general well-being. They can also be used for estate planning, allowing individuals to transfer their wealth to future generations while minimizing estate taxes.

It's important to note that setting up and managing a trust fund requires careful consideration and professional guidance. However, with the right knowledge and support, regular individuals can leverage trust funds to enhance their financial security and achieve their long-term goals.

- Explain the different types of trust funds and their purposes

There are several different types of trust funds, each with its own specific purpose and benefits. Here are some of the most common types:

1. Revocable Living Trust: This type of trust allows individuals to maintain control over their assets during their lifetime while providing for the seamless transfer of those assets to beneficiaries upon their death. It can help avoid probate, a legal process that can be time-consuming and expensive.

2. Irrevocable Trust: Unlike a revocable living trust, an irrevocable trust cannot be changed or revoked once it's established. This type of trust is often used for tax planning purposes, asset protection, and Medicaid planning. By transferring assets into an irrevocable trust, individuals can reduce their taxable estate and protect assets from creditors.

3. Testamentary Trust: This trust is created through a person's will and takes effect upon their death. It allows individuals to specify how their assets will be distributed to beneficiaries, providing control over how and when the assets are used. Testamentary trusts are often used to provide for minor children or individuals with special needs.

4. Charitable Trust: A charitable trust is established to benefit a charitable organization or cause. It allows individuals to make a lasting impact by providing ongoing financial support to their chosen charity. Charitable trusts can also offer tax advantages, such as income tax deductions and reduced estate taxes.

5. Special Needs Trust: This trust is designed to provide for the financial needs of a person with disabilities without jeopardizing

their eligibility for government benefits. It allows individuals to set aside funds for the care and support of their loved ones with special needs while ensuring their access to essential government assistance programs.

6. Spendthrift Trust: A spendthrift trust is created to protect the assets of a beneficiary from their own poor financial decisions or potential creditors. It allows the trustee to have control over the distribution of funds, ensuring that the beneficiary's financial well-being is protected.

These are just a few examples of the different types of trust funds available. The choice of trust type depends on individual goals, financial circumstances, and the intended beneficiaries. It's important to consult with a legal or financial professional to determine the most suitable trust fund structure for your specific needs.

- Address common misconceptions and dispel myths surrounding trust funds

Trust funds have gained a reputation for being exclusive financial tools only for the wealthy or for complex estate planning. However, it's important to address common misconceptions and dispel some myths surrounding trust funds. Here are a few:

1. Myth: Trust funds are only for the super-rich.
   Reality: Trust funds are not exclusive to the super-rich. While they can be used by high-net-worth individuals, trust funds are also beneficial for individuals with more modest assets. Trusts can be customized to fit different financial situations and goals.

2. Myth: Trust funds are only for old people.
   Reality: Trust funds can benefit individuals of any age. They can be used to protect assets, provide for loved ones, and plan for the future. Establishing a trust fund early in life can help individuals ensure their assets are managed and distributed according to their wishes.

3. Myth: Trust funds are complicated and expensive to set up.

Reality: While setting up a trust fund does require careful consideration and professional guidance, it doesn't have to be overly complicated or prohibitively expensive. Trust structures can be tailored to fit individual needs and budgets. Working with an experienced attorney or financial advisor can help simplify the process.

4. Myth: Trust funds are only for passing down wealth to future generations.
    Reality: While trust funds are commonly used for estate planning and passing down wealth, they can serve a variety of purposes. Trust funds can be used to provide for education, healthcare, charitable giving, or support individuals with special needs. They can also be used for personal asset protection and tax planning.

5. Myth: Trust funds are only for individuals with complex family situations.
    Reality: While trust funds can be beneficial in complex family situations, such as blended families or individuals with multiple dependents, they can also provide advantages for individuals with more straightforward family structures. Trusts can help ensure assets are distributed according to an individual's wishes, regardless of family dynamics.

It's important to consult with legal and financial professionals to understand the benefits, costs, and implications of setting up a trust fund. They can help dispel any misconceptions and tailor a trust structure that aligns with your specific goals and circumstances.

Chapter 2: Laying the Groundwork: Preparing for Your Trust Fund Journey

- Assess readers' financial goals and motivations for setting up a trust fund

1. Estate Planning: Many individuals establish trust funds as part of their estate planning strategy. They want to ensure that their assets are managed and distributed according to their wishes after their passing. Trusts can provide control over how and when assets are distributed, minimize estate taxes, and avoid probate.

2. Asset Protection: Some individuals set up trust funds to protect their assets from potential risks, such as lawsuits, creditors, or divorce. By placing assets in a trust, they can shield them from being easily accessed or seized by third parties.

3. Providing for Loved Ones: Trust funds can be used to provide ongoing financial support to loved ones, such as children, grandchildren, or individuals with special needs. It allows individuals to ensure that their beneficiaries are taken care of, even after they are gone.

4. Tax Planning: Trusts can offer tax advantages, depending on the specific structure and purpose. They can help reduce estate taxes, income taxes, or capital gains taxes. Individuals may consider setting up a trust to optimize their tax planning strategies.

5. Charitable Giving: Trust funds can be established to support charitable causes and organizations. They allow individuals to make a lasting impact by providing ongoing financial support to their chosen charities or causes.

6. Business Succession Planning: Trusts can be utilized for business owners who want to plan for the smooth transfer of their business to the next generation or a designated successor. It can help ensure the continuity and success of the business.

These are just a few examples of the motivations individuals may have for setting up a trust fund. It's essential for individuals to assess their own financial goals, consult with professionals, and consider their unique circumstances when determining if a trust fund aligns with their needs.

- Guide readers in evaluating their financial situation and readiness for a trust fund

Evaluating your financial situation and readiness for a trust fund is an important step before deciding to establish one. Here are some key factors to consider:

1. Financial Stability: Assess your financial stability and whether you have sufficient assets to warrant the creation of a trust fund. Trust funds can involve costs for setting up and maintaining, so it's essential to ensure you have the financial resources to support it.

2. Financial Goals: Determine your financial goals and how a trust fund aligns with them. Are you primarily focused on estate planning, asset protection, providing for loved ones, or achieving specific tax benefits? Understanding your objectives will help you determine if a trust fund is the right tool for you.

3. Asset Ownership: Evaluate the types of assets you own and whether they are suitable for inclusion in a trust. Assets such as real estate, investments, business interests, and valuable personal property can be placed in a trust. On the other hand, liquid assets or assets that require regular access may not be ideal for a trust structure.

4. Family and Beneficiaries: Consider your family dynamics and potential beneficiaries. Are there specific individuals or groups you want to provide for through the trust fund? Assess the needs and circumstances of your loved ones to determine if a trust is an appropriate vehicle for addressing their financial well-being.

5. Professional Guidance: Consult with legal and financial professionals who specialize in trusts and estate planning. They can assess your financial situation, goals, and provide tailored advice based on your specific needs. They will help you understand the legal and tax implications, as well as guide you through the process of setting up and managing a trust fund.

6. Time Horizon: Consider your time horizon for the trust fund. Trusts can be established for short-term or long-term purposes. Evaluate whether you have a clear vision for how long you want the trust to last and what outcomes you hope to achieve during that time.

7. Cost-Benefit Analysis: Conduct a cost-benefit analysis to determine if the benefits of establishing a trust fund outweigh the associated costs. Consider the expenses involved in setting up and maintaining the trust, as well as any potential tax savings or other advantages it may offer.

By carefully evaluating these factors and seeking professional guidance, you can determine if you are financially ready for a trust fund. Remember, each person's financial situation is unique, so it's important to consider your specific circumstances and goals before making a decision.

- Provide tips and resources for gathering the necessary documentation and information

Gathering the necessary documentation and information is a crucial step in the process of setting up a trust fund. Here are some tips and resources to help you with this task:

1. Consult with Professionals: Engage the services of an experienced attorney specializing in trusts and estates. They can guide you through the documentation requirements and provide you with a checklist of the necessary documents based on your specific circumstances.

2. Identify Trustees and Beneficiaries: Make a list of potential trustees and beneficiaries who will be involved in the trust. Gather their contact information, social security numbers, and any other relevant details.

3. Financial Statements: Collect your financial statements, including bank account statements, investment account statements, retirement account statements, and any other relevant financial documents. These statements will help determine the value of your assets and provide a clear picture of your financial situation.

4. Property and Asset Documentation: Gather documentation related to your properties and assets, such as real estate deeds, vehicle titles, stock certificates, business ownership documents, and any other

proof of ownership. These documents will be used to transfer ownership to the trust.

5. Estate Planning Documents: If you have any existing estate planning documents, such as a will or power of attorney, gather them for review by your attorney. These documents may need to be updated or revised to align with the trust structure.

6. Personal Information: Prepare personal information for yourself, trustees, and beneficiaries. This includes full legal names, dates of birth, social security numbers, addresses, and contact information. This information is necessary for legal and administrative purposes.

7. Insurance Policies: Collect copies of any life insurance policies, disability insurance policies, or long-term care insurance policies you may have. These policies may have an impact on the trust fund and should be reviewed by your attorney.

8. Business Documents: If you own a business or have interests in a business, gather relevant business documents, such as partnership agreements, operating agreements, and financial statements. These documents will help determine the value and ownership structure of the business assets.

9. Tax Information: Compile your tax documents, including income tax returns, gift tax returns, and any other relevant tax filings. These documents will assist your attorney in understanding your tax situation and developing an appropriate trust strategy.

10. Online Resources: Various online resources provide templates and checklists for gathering trust fund documentation. Some reputable sources include legal websites, estate planning organizations, or government websites that provide information on trusts and estate planning.

Remember, the specific documents and information required may vary depending on your unique circumstances and the type of trust you are establishing. It's always recommended to consult with a qualified attorney who can provide you with personalized guidance and ensure all necessary documentation is gathered.

Chapter 3: Choosing the Right Trust Fund: Finding Your Perfect Fit

- Discuss the various types of trust funds available to regular individuals

There are several types of trust funds available to regular individuals, each designed to serve different purposes and meet specific needs. Here are some of the most common types:

1. Revocable Living Trust: A revocable living trust is created during the grantor's lifetime and can be modified or revoked at any time. It allows the grantor to retain control over the assets placed in the trust while providing a mechanism for the seamless transfer of assets to beneficiaries upon the grantor's death. This type of trust can help avoid probate and maintain privacy.

2. Irrevocable Trust: An irrevocable trust, as the name suggests, cannot be modified or revoked once established, except under certain circumstances. This type of trust transfers ownership of assets out of the grantor's control, providing potential benefits such as asset protection, estate tax reduction, and eligibility for certain government benefits.

3. Testamentary Trust: A testamentary trust is created through a will and takes effect after the grantor's death. This type of trust allows the grantor to specify how their assets should be managed and distributed to beneficiaries. Testamentary trusts are often used to provide for minor children or individuals with special needs.

4. Special Needs Trust: A special needs trust is designed to provide for the needs of individuals with disabilities without jeopardizing their eligibility for government benefits. This type of trust allows assets to be used for the beneficiary's supplemental needs that are not covered by government assistance programs.

5. Charitable Trust: A charitable trust is established to benefit a charitable organization or cause. It allows individuals to donate

assets while providing potential tax benefits. Charitable trusts can be structured to provide income to the donor during their lifetime and then distribute the remaining assets to the designated charity upon their death.

6. Spendthrift Trust: A spendthrift trust is created to protect the assets of a beneficiary from creditors or the beneficiary's own poor financial decisions. The trust controls the distribution of funds, providing regular payments to the beneficiary while ensuring the assets remain protected.

7. Educational Trust: An educational trust is established to fund the education expenses of a beneficiary. It can be used to save for a child's college education or provide ongoing support for educational pursuits.

8. Family Trust: A family trust is created to benefit multiple generations of a family. It can be used to manage and distribute family assets, provide for the financial well-being of family members, and facilitate estate planning goals.

These are just a few examples of the types of trust funds available to regular individuals. It's important to consult with a qualified attorney or financial advisor to determine which type of trust is most suitable for your specific needs and goals. They can provide personalized guidance based on your circumstances and help you establish the appropriate trust structure.

- Explain the differences between revocable and irrevocable trusts, and their respective benefits

Revocable and irrevocable trusts are two distinct types of trusts that offer different levels of control and flexibility to the grantor. Here are the key differences between revocable and irrevocable trusts, along with their respective benefits:

1. Revocable Trust:
   - Flexibility: A revocable trust, also known as a living trust, can be modified, amended, or revoked by the grantor during their lifetime. This provides flexibility in managing and controlling the trust assets.

- Probate Avoidance: One of the primary benefits of a revocable trust is that it helps avoid probate, the legal process of distributing assets after a person's death. By transferring assets into the trust, they are considered outside of the grantor's probate estate, which can save time and costs.
- Privacy: Revocable trusts offer a higher level of privacy compared to wills. Since they do not go through probate, the terms and details of the trust remain private.
- Incapacity Planning: A revocable trust can include provisions for managing assets in case the grantor becomes incapacitated. It allows for a smooth transition of control to a successor trustee without the need for court intervention.

2. Irrevocable Trust:
- Asset Protection: One of the primary benefits of an irrevocable trust is asset protection. Once assets are transferred into an irrevocable trust, they are no longer considered part of the grantor's estate and are shielded from creditors and legal claims.
- Estate Tax Reduction: Irrevocable trusts can be used as an estate planning tool to reduce estate taxes. By transferring assets into an irrevocable trust, the grantor effectively removes the assets from their taxable estate, potentially reducing the estate tax burden.
- Medicaid Planning: An irrevocable trust can be structured to help individuals qualify for Medicaid benefits while preserving assets. By transferring assets into the trust, the grantor may meet the eligibility criteria for Medicaid without depleting their assets.
- Charitable Giving: Irrevocable trusts can be used to support charitable causes. By establishing a charitable trust, the grantor can make a lasting impact while potentially receiving tax benefits.

It's important to note that once an irrevocable trust is established, the grantor generally relinquishes control over the assets and cannot make changes without the consent of the beneficiaries or a court order. Revocable trusts, on the other hand, allow the grantor to retain control and make changes as needed.

Both types of trusts have their advantages and considerations. It's crucial to consult with an experienced attorney or financial advisor to determine which type of trust aligns with your specific goals, financial situation, and estate planning needs. They can provide personalized guidance and assist you in creating the appropriate trust structure.

- Help readers determine the most suitable trust fund structure for their specific needs and circumstances

Determining the most suitable trust fund structure for specific needs and circumstances requires careful consideration of various factors. Here are some steps to help readers determine the best trust fund structure for their situation:

1. Identify Goals and Objectives: Start by clearly defining your goals and objectives for establishing a trust. Consider what you want to achieve with the trust, such as asset protection, tax planning, providing for loved ones, or supporting charitable causes.

2. Assess Financial Situation: Evaluate your current financial situation, including your assets, liabilities, income, and expenses. Understanding your financial picture will help determine the type and size of the trust fund that aligns with your resources.

3. Consider Family and Beneficiaries: Think about your family dynamics and the needs of your beneficiaries. If you have minor children, individuals with special needs, or family members with specific financial circumstances, you may need a trust structure tailored to address their unique requirements.

4. Evaluate Risk Factors: Assess potential risks and challenges that may impact your assets or beneficiaries. Consider factors such as creditor protection, potential lawsuits, divorce, or financial irresponsibility. Identifying and addressing these risks can guide you towards the appropriate trust structure.

5. Consult Professionals: Seek guidance from professionals with expertise in trust and estate planning, such as attorneys and financial advisors. They can provide personalized advice based on your specific circumstances and help navigate the complexities of trust fund structures.

6. Understand Different Trust Types: Familiarize yourself with the various types of trusts available, such as revocable trusts, irrevocable trusts, testamentary trusts, special needs trusts, and charitable trusts. Learn about their features, benefits, and limitations to determine which ones align with your goals.

7. Balance Control and Flexibility: Consider your preferences for control and flexibility over the trust assets. Revocable trusts offer more control but may have limitations in terms of asset protection and tax planning, while irrevocable trusts provide greater asset protection but have less flexibility.

8. Review Tax Implications: Understand the potential tax implications of different trust structures. Consult with a tax advisor to assess the impact on income taxes, estate taxes, gift taxes, and generation-skipping transfer taxes.

9. Review Legal Requirements: Familiarize yourself with the legal requirements and formalities associated with establishing and maintaining a trust. Different jurisdictions may have specific rules and regulations that need to be followed.

10. Regularly Review and Update: Keep in mind that circumstances change over time, so it's essential to regularly review and update your trust fund structure to ensure it continues to meet your evolving needs and goals.

Remember, each individual's situation is unique, and what works for one person may not work for another. It's crucial to seek professional advice tailored to your specific needs and circumstances to determine the most suitable trust fund structure.

Chapter 4: Setting Up Your Trust Fund: Step-by-Step Instructions

- Provide a detailed, easy-to-follow guide on establishing a trust fund

Establishing a trust fund involves several steps and considerations. Here is a detailed, easy-to-follow guide to help you navigate the process:

Step 1: Determine Your Goals and Objectives
- Clearly define your goals for establishing a trust fund. Consider what you want to achieve, such as asset protection, tax planning, providing for loved ones, or supporting charitable causes.

Step 2: Choose the Type of Trust
- Understand the different types of trusts available, such as revocable trusts, irrevocable trusts, testamentary trusts, special needs trusts, and charitable trusts. Choose the type that aligns with your goals and circumstances.

Step 3: Seek Professional Guidance
- Consult with an experienced attorney who specializes in trust and estate planning. They can provide personalized advice based on your specific needs and guide you through the legal requirements.

Step 4: Identify Trustees and Beneficiaries
- Determine who will serve as the trustee(s) responsible for managing the trust assets and making distributions. Also, identify the beneficiaries who will receive the benefits from the trust.

Step 5: Draft the Trust Document
- Work with your attorney to draft the trust document. This document outlines the terms, conditions, and instructions for the trust. It should include details such as the trust's purpose, assets to be included, trustee powers and responsibilities, and beneficiary provisions.

Step 6: Fund the Trust
- Transfer assets into the trust. This may involve retitling assets, changing ownership, or assigning ownership rights to the trust. Consult with your attorney or financial advisor to ensure the proper transfer of assets.

Step 7: Consider Tax Implications

- Understand the potential tax implications of the trust fund. Consult with a tax advisor to assess the impact on income taxes, estate taxes, gift taxes, and generation-skipping transfer taxes.

Step 8: Review and Update Regularly
- Regularly review and update the trust fund as circumstances change. Ensure that the trust remains aligned with your goals, accounts for any changes in beneficiaries or trustees, and complies with any legal or tax updates.

Step 9: Communicate and Educate
- Clearly communicate the existence and purpose of the trust to the trustees and beneficiaries. Provide them with necessary information and education regarding their roles, rights, and responsibilities.

Step 10: Monitor and Manage the Trust
- Regularly monitor the performance of the trust and its assets. Work closely with the trustee(s) to ensure the trust is managed effectively and in line with your objectives.

Remember, establishing a trust fund is a complex legal process, and it's crucial to seek professional advice from an experienced attorney. They can provide guidance tailored to your specific needs, ensure compliance with legal requirements, and help you create a trust fund structure that aligns with your goals and objectives.

- Explain the legal and financial considerations involved in the setup process

The setup process for a trust fund involves several legal and financial considerations. Here are some key aspects to keep in mind:

Legal Considerations:
1. Trust Laws: Understand the trust laws in your jurisdiction. Each jurisdiction may have specific rules and regulations governing the creation and administration of trusts. Familiarize yourself with these laws to ensure compliance.

2. Trust Document: Work with an attorney to draft the trust document. This legal document outlines the terms and conditions of

the trust, including the purpose, trustee powers, beneficiary provisions, and distribution instructions. It is essential to ensure that the trust document accurately reflects your intentions and complies with legal requirements.

3. Selection of Trustees: Choose trustworthy individuals or professional entities to serve as trustees. Trustees have legal obligations and responsibilities to manage the trust assets and make distributions according to the trust document. Ensure they have the necessary qualifications and expertise to fulfill their duties.

4. Beneficiary Designations: Clearly identify the beneficiaries who will receive the benefits from the trust. Specify their rights, entitlements, and any conditions or restrictions associated with their distributions.

5. Formalities and Execution: Follow the legal formalities and execution requirements when establishing the trust. This may include signing and notarizing the trust document and complying with any additional legal procedures mandated by your jurisdiction.

Financial Considerations:
1. Funding the Trust: Transfer assets into the trust fund. This may involve retitling assets, changing ownership, or assigning ownership rights to the trust. Consult with your financial advisor or attorney to ensure the proper transfer of assets and to consider any tax implications.

2. Asset Management: Determine how the trust assets will be managed. This may involve investment decisions, selecting investment advisors, and establishing an investment strategy aligned with the trust's goals and risk tolerance.

3. Tax Planning: Consider the tax implications of the trust fund. Consult with a tax advisor to understand how the trust will be taxed, including income taxes, estate taxes, gift taxes, and generation-skipping transfer taxes. Explore strategies to optimize tax efficiency and minimize tax liabilities.

4. Regular Reviews and Updates: Regularly review the trust fund's performance and financial situation. Assess whether adjustments need to be made to the asset allocation, investment strategy, or distribution provisions. Stay informed about changes in tax laws or regulations that may impact the trust.

5. Accounting and Record-Keeping: Maintain accurate accounting records of the trust's financial activities, including income, expenses, investments, and distributions. Adhere to proper record-keeping practices to ensure transparency and compliance with legal and tax requirements.

It is crucial to consult with professionals, such as attorneys and financial advisors, who specialize in trust and estate planning. They can provide expert guidance tailored to your specific circumstances, help navigate the legal and financial complexities, and ensure that the trust fund is established and managed effectively.

- Offer practical tips for selecting trustees and beneficiaries

When selecting trustees and beneficiaries for a trust fund, it's important to consider various factors to ensure the smooth administration and success of the trust. Here are some practical tips to guide you in the selection process:

Selecting Trustees:
1. Trustworthiness and Integrity: Choose individuals or professional entities who possess a high level of trustworthiness and integrity. Trustees will have significant control over the trust assets and making distributions, so it's crucial to select someone who will act in the best interests of the beneficiaries and fulfill their fiduciary duties.

2. Competence and Expertise: Look for trustees who have the necessary competence and expertise to manage the trust assets effectively. They should have a good understanding of financial management, investment strategies, and legal responsibilities associated with being a trustee. Consider their professional qualifications and experience in trust administration.

3. Communication and Collaboration: Prioritize trustees who demonstrate effective communication skills and the ability to collaborate with beneficiaries, other trustees, and professionals involved in trust administration. Clear and open communication is essential for a smooth and transparent trust administration process.

4. Availability and Longevity: Consider the availability and longevity of potential trustees. Trustees should be willing and able to serve for the duration of the trust's existence. Select individuals who have the time and commitment to fulfill their trustee responsibilities and who will be available to address any future needs or changes that may arise.

Selecting Beneficiaries:
1. Clarity of Purpose: Clearly define the purpose and objectives of the trust to determine the appropriate beneficiaries. Identify individuals or groups who align with the intended purpose of the trust and who will benefit from the trust's assets and provisions.

2. Relationship and Dependence: Consider the relationship and level of dependence between potential beneficiaries and the trust creator. Assess their financial needs, circumstances, and their ability to responsibly manage the assets or benefits they will receive from the trust.

3. Age and Maturity: Take into account the age and maturity of potential beneficiaries. Consider whether they are of legal age to receive trust distributions or if additional safeguards, such as a trust protector, may be necessary to manage distributions until beneficiaries reach a certain age or level of maturity.

4. Special Considerations: If there are specific considerations, such as special needs or charitable intentions, choose beneficiaries who will benefit most from the trust assets and provisions. Ensure that the trust provisions adequately address their unique circumstances and requirements.

5. Succession Planning: Plan for contingencies and consider future generations when selecting beneficiaries. Anticipate potential

changes in family dynamics or circumstances and establish a clear process for adding or removing beneficiaries as needed.

Remember to consult with your attorney or professional advisors when selecting trustees and beneficiaries. They can provide personalized guidance based on your specific goals and circumstances, ensuring that your choices align with your objectives and comply with legal requirements.

Chapter 5: Protecting Your Wealth: Safeguarding Assets and Minimizing Risk

- Explore how trust funds provide asset protection and shield wealth from potential threats

Trust funds can offer significant asset protection and serve as a valuable tool for shielding wealth from potential threats. Here's how trust funds can provide asset protection:

1. Creditor Protection: One of the primary benefits of a trust fund is that it can provide a layer of protection against creditors. By transferring assets to a trust, those assets are no longer considered part of the individual's personal estate. As a result, they may be shielded from potential claims or legal actions by creditors seeking to collect debts.

2. Lawsuit Protection: Trust funds can help safeguard assets from potential lawsuits. When assets are placed in a properly structured trust, they are held separately from the individual's personal ownership. In the event of a lawsuit, the trust assets may be protected from being seized or used to satisfy legal judgments.

3. Divorce Protection: Trust funds can play a role in protecting assets in the event of a divorce. By establishing a trust and transferring assets into it, those assets may be shielded from being subject to division as part of the marital assets. This can help ensure that the

intended beneficiaries retain control and ownership of the trust assets.

4. Privacy Protection: Trust funds offer a level of privacy for individuals seeking to shield their wealth. Unlike wills, which become public documents upon death, trust documents generally remain private. This means that the details of the trust, including the specific assets and beneficiaries, can be kept confidential.

5. Generational Wealth Transfer: Trust funds can be structured to facilitate the efficient transfer of wealth across multiple generations. By establishing a trust, individuals can designate how and when assets are distributed to beneficiaries. This can help protect the family's wealth from being eroded due to poor financial decisions, creditor claims, or other threats.

6. Tax Planning: Trust funds can provide tax advantages and help minimize tax liabilities. Depending on the jurisdiction and specific trust structure, individuals may be able to take advantage of tax benefits such as estate tax reduction, gift tax savings, and income tax planning strategies. Consult with a tax advisor or estate planning attorney to explore tax-efficient trust structures.

It's important to note that the effectiveness of asset protection strategies can vary depending on the jurisdiction and specific circumstances. Laws governing trusts and asset protection can differ, so it's crucial to consult with legal and financial professionals who specialize in trust and estate planning to ensure that the chosen trust structure aligns with your objectives and provides the desired asset protection.

- Discuss strategies for minimizing risk and protecting assets from litigation, creditors, and other risks

Minimizing risk and protecting assets from litigation, creditors, and other risks is an important aspect of wealth management and asset protection. Here are some strategies to consider:

1. Establishing Trusts: Trusts, such as revocable living trusts or irrevocable trusts, can be effective tools for protecting assets. By

transferring assets into a trust, they are held separately from personal ownership and may be shielded from potential claims by creditors or legal actions.

2. Limited Liability Entities: Structuring assets within limited liability entities, such as limited liability companies (LLCs) or limited partnerships (LPs), can provide an additional layer of protection. These entities can help shield personal assets from liabilities associated with business ventures or investments.

3. Asset Segregation: Segregating assets into different legal entities or accounts can help protect them from potential risks. By keeping assets separate, a problem with one asset or entity is less likely to affect the entire portfolio. This strategy can help minimize exposure and limit the potential impact of litigation or creditor claims.

4. Insurance Coverage: Maintaining adequate insurance coverage is essential for managing risk and protecting assets. Liability insurance, including umbrella policies, can provide an additional layer of protection in case of lawsuits or other claims. Property and casualty insurance can help cover potential losses due to events like theft, fire, or natural disasters.

5. Homestead Exemptions: Taking advantage of homestead exemptions, available in some jurisdictions, can protect a primary residence from creditors. Homestead laws vary by state and typically provide a certain level of protection for a person's primary residence.

6. Business Succession Planning: Implementing a well-structured business succession plan can help protect business assets and ensure a smooth transition of ownership. By planning for the future and documenting the transfer of ownership, the risk of disputes or disruptions to the business can be minimized.

7. Regular Risk Assessment: Conducting regular risk assessments of personal and business assets is crucial. Identifying potential risks and vulnerabilities allows for proactive measures to be taken to mitigate those risks. This can involve reviewing contracts, updating legal

documents, and implementing safeguards to protect against identified risks.

8. Professional Guidance: Seeking advice from legal and financial professionals who specialize in asset protection and risk management is essential. These professionals can provide personalized guidance based on your specific circumstances and help design strategies that align with your goals and comply with applicable laws and regulations.

It's important to note that asset protection strategies should be implemented proactively, before any potential threats or risks arise. Engaging in fraudulent activities or using asset protection strategies with the intent to defraud creditors is illegal and can result in legal consequences. Consult with professionals to ensure that your asset protection strategies are implemented ethically and in compliance with the law.

- Highlight real-life case studies illustrating the benefits of trust funds in safeguarding wealth

Here are a few real-life case studies that demonstrate the benefits of trust funds in safeguarding wealth:

1. The Rockefeller Family: The Rockefeller family is renowned for their successful use of trust funds to preserve and protect their wealth for generations. In the late 19th century, John D. Rockefeller established a trust fund, known as the Rockefeller Foundation, which allowed him to transfer a significant portion of his wealth to future generations. The trust fund provided asset protection, ensured the philanthropic goals of the family were met, and helped preserve their wealth over time.

2. Warren Buffett: Warren Buffett, one of the world's most successful investors, has also utilized trust funds to protect his wealth. He established the Susan Thompson Buffett Foundation, named after his late wife, to manage and distribute his wealth for charitable purposes. By placing his assets in a trust, Buffett ensured

that his wealth would be used for philanthropic endeavors, while also providing a level of asset protection and privacy.

3. Sam Walton and the Walton Family: The Walton family, founders of Walmart, have utilized trust funds to protect their wealth and plan for the future. Sam Walton established the Walton Family Holdings Trust, which holds a significant portion of the family's Walmart shares. This trust allows for the efficient transfer of wealth to future generations, while also providing asset protection and minimizing estate taxes.

4. Bill and Melinda Gates: Bill and Melinda Gates established the Bill & Melinda Gates Foundation, one of the largest charitable foundations in the world. By transferring a substantial amount of their wealth to the foundation, they were able to protect their assets, ensure the continuation of their philanthropic efforts, and maintain a level of privacy. The foundation's structure as a trust allows for the effective management and distribution of their wealth for charitable purposes.

These case studies highlight how trust funds have been utilized by wealthy individuals and families to safeguard their wealth, protect assets from potential threats, and facilitate long-term planning. Trust funds offer a range of benefits, including asset protection, privacy, efficient wealth transfer, and the ability to support philanthropic goals. However, it's important to note that trust funds are not limited to the ultra-wealthy and can be a valuable tool for individuals seeking to protect their assets and plan for the future.

Chapter 6: Tax Advantage Strategies: Maximizing Returns and Minimizing Taxes

- Explain the tax advantages associated with trust funds for regular individuals

Trust funds can provide several tax advantages for regular individuals. Here are some of the tax benefits associated with trust funds:

1. Estate Tax Reduction: One of the primary tax advantages of trust funds is the potential reduction of estate taxes. When assets are transferred into a trust, they are no longer considered part of the individual's estate for tax purposes. This can help minimize the estate tax liability upon the individual's death, allowing more of the wealth to pass on to beneficiaries.

2. Gift Tax Exemption: Trust funds can also be used to take advantage of gift tax exemptions. By transferring assets into a trust and designating beneficiaries, individuals can make gifts that are excluded from gift tax calculations. This can be particularly beneficial for individuals who want to transfer assets to their loved ones during their lifetime while minimizing gift tax implications.

3. Income Tax Planning: Trust funds can offer income tax planning opportunities. Depending on the type of trust, income earned by the trust may be taxed at a lower rate compared to the individual's personal income tax rate. This can help optimize tax efficiency and potentially reduce the overall tax burden.

4. Step-Up in Basis: In certain cases, trust funds can provide a step-up in basis for assets held in the trust. When assets are transferred into a trust, they are revalued at their fair market value as of the date of transfer. This can result in a higher cost basis for the assets, potentially reducing capital gains taxes when the assets are eventually sold.

5. Generation-Skipping Transfer Tax Exemption: Trust funds can also facilitate the transfer of wealth to future generations while minimizing generation-skipping transfer taxes. Generation-skipping transfer taxes are imposed when assets are transferred to individuals who are more than one generation below the transferor. Trusts can be structured to take advantage of exemptions and minimize the impact of these taxes.

It's important to note that the tax advantages associated with trust funds can vary depending on the individual's specific circumstances, the type of trust, and applicable tax laws. It's always recommended to consult with a qualified tax professional or estate planning attorney to understand the tax implications and benefits of establishing a trust fund based on your unique situation.

- Provide a comprehensive overview of tax planning strategies to optimize wealth growth

Tax planning strategies can play a crucial role in optimizing wealth growth by minimizing tax liabilities and maximizing after-tax returns. Here is a comprehensive overview of various tax planning strategies that can help individuals and businesses optimize their wealth growth:

1. Retirement Account Contributions: Contributing to tax-advantaged retirement accounts, such as 401(k)s, IRAs, or SEP-IRAs, can offer immediate tax benefits. Contributions to these accounts are typically tax-deductible, reducing taxable income and allowing for tax-deferred growth.

2. Tax-Loss Harvesting: Tax-loss harvesting involves selling investments that have experienced a loss to offset capital gains and reduce taxable income. This strategy can help individuals minimize their tax liability while rebalancing their investment portfolios.

3. Asset Location: By strategically locating different types of investments in taxable and tax-advantaged accounts, individuals can optimize their tax efficiency. Tax-efficient investments, such as index funds or tax-managed funds, can be held in taxable accounts, while tax-inefficient investments, like bonds or actively managed funds, can be held in tax-advantaged accounts to minimize the tax impact.

4. Charitable Giving: Donating to qualified charitable organizations not only supports causes individuals care about but also provides tax benefits. Charitable contributions can be deducted from taxable income, reducing the overall tax liability.

5. Tax-Efficient Investing: Implementing tax-efficient investment strategies can help individuals minimize the tax consequences of investment activities. This can include strategies like holding investments for more than one year to qualify for long-term capital gains rates or investing in tax-efficient funds that minimize taxable distributions.

6. Estate Planning: Proper estate planning can help minimize estate taxes and ensure the smooth transfer of wealth to future generations. Strategies such as gifting assets, establishing trusts, and utilizing life insurance policies can help reduce estate tax liabilities.

7. Business Expense Deductions: Business owners can take advantage of various deductions to reduce their taxable income. This can include deductions for business-related expenses such as salaries, rent, equipment, and travel.

8. Tax Credits: Tax credits directly reduce the tax liability and can be highly beneficial in optimizing wealth growth. Examples of tax credits include the Earned Income Tax Credit, Child Tax Credit, and energy-efficient home improvement credits.

9. Education Savings Plans: Utilizing education savings plans, such as 529 plans or Coverdell Education Savings Accounts, can provide tax advantages for saving for future education expenses. Contributions to these plans may be tax-deductible, and the earnings grow tax-free when used for qualified education expenses.

10. Health Savings Accounts (HSAs): HSAs offer triple tax benefits. Contributions are tax-deductible, earnings grow tax-free, and withdrawals for qualified medical expenses are tax-free. HSAs can be a powerful tool for managing healthcare costs and optimizing tax savings.

It's important to note that tax planning strategies should be implemented in line with applicable tax laws and regulations. Consulting with a qualified tax professional or financial advisor is recommended to ensure that these strategies are tailored to individual circumstances and objectives.

Overall, by employing these tax planning strategies effectively, individuals and businesses can minimize their tax liabilities, maximize after-tax returns, and ultimately optimize their wealth growth.

- Offer insights on utilizing trust funds to minimize taxes and maximize investment returns

Utilizing trust funds can provide individuals with opportunities to minimize taxes and maximize investment returns. Here are some insights on how trust funds can be used for tax optimization and investment growth:

1. Tax Planning with Irrevocable Trusts: Irrevocable trusts can be an effective tool for minimizing taxes. By transferring assets into an irrevocable trust, individuals can remove those assets from their taxable estate, potentially reducing estate taxes. Additionally, income generated by the trust can be taxed at the trust level, which may result in lower tax rates compared to individual income tax rates.

2. Grantor Retained Annuity Trusts (GRATs): GRATs allow individuals to transfer appreciating assets into a trust while retaining an annuity payment for a specific term. At the end of the term, any remaining assets in the trust pass to the beneficiaries. By carefully structuring a GRAT, individuals can potentially transfer assets with minimal or no gift tax implications, thus minimizing taxes while allowing for investment growth within the trust.

3. Dynasty Trusts: Dynasty trusts are designed to provide long-term wealth preservation and growth for multiple generations. By utilizing the generation-skipping transfer tax exemption, individuals can transfer assets to a dynasty trust, allowing for tax-free growth and minimizing taxes that would apply if the assets were transferred directly to future generations.

4. Charitable Remainder Trusts (CRTs): CRTs allow individuals to donate assets to a trust while retaining an income stream for a specific period or their lifetime. By donating appreciated assets to a

CRT, individuals can receive a charitable income tax deduction, potentially reduce estate taxes, and defer capital gains taxes on the donated assets. This strategy allows individuals to support charitable causes while optimizing tax benefits and potentially increasing investment returns.

5. Qualified Personal Residence Trusts (QPRTs): QPRTs enable individuals to transfer their primary residence or vacation home into a trust while retaining the right to live in the property for a specific term. By transferring the property at a reduced value, individuals can potentially minimize gift and estate taxes. This strategy allows for tax-efficient transfer of real estate assets while still enjoying the use of the property.

6. Investment Strategies within Trusts: Trusts provide flexibility in investment management, allowing for diversification and potential growth. Trustees can invest trust assets in a variety of investment vehicles, such as stocks, bonds, real estate, and mutual funds, based on the trust's investment objectives and risk tolerance. By carefully selecting investment options and regularly reviewing the trust's investment performance, individuals can maximize investment returns within the trust.

7. Tax-Efficient Distributions: Trustees can manage trust distributions in a tax-efficient manner. By strategically timing distributions and considering the tax implications for beneficiaries, trustees can minimize tax liabilities for both the trust and its beneficiaries. This may involve coordinating distributions with beneficiaries' income levels or leveraging tax brackets to optimize tax outcomes.

It's important to note that utilizing trust funds for tax optimization and investment growth requires careful planning and consideration of legal and tax implications. Consulting with a qualified estate planning attorney and financial advisor is recommended to ensure that trust structures align with individual circumstances and goals.

Overall, trust funds can be powerful tools for minimizing taxes and maximizing investment returns. By leveraging various types of trusts and employing strategic tax and investment strategies, individuals can optimize their wealth growth while maintaining control and flexibility over their assets.

Chapter 7: Ensuring Your Family's Future: Securing Financial Stability

- Discuss how trust funds can provide financial security for loved ones

Trust funds can be an effective means of providing financial security for loved ones. By establishing a trust and carefully structuring its terms, individuals can ensure that their assets are managed and distributed in accordance with their wishes, while also providing ongoing financial support. Here are some key ways in which trust funds can provide financial security for loved ones:

1. Asset Protection: One of the primary benefits of a trust is that it can help protect assets from various risks. By placing assets in a trust, individuals can shield them from potential creditors, lawsuits, or other claims. This ensures that the assets are preserved and available for the benefit of loved ones.

2. Controlled Distribution: Trusts allow individuals to specify how and when assets are distributed to beneficiaries. This can be particularly useful when beneficiaries are minors, have special needs, or lack financial management skills. The trust can provide for regular distributions, lump-sum payments, or specific purposes (e.g., education, healthcare) as outlined by the grantor.

3. Long-Term Support: Trust funds can provide ongoing financial support for loved ones, ensuring their well-being over the long term. For example, a trust can be structured to provide regular income payments or cover specific expenses, such as housing, healthcare, education, or other essential needs. This can provide peace of mind knowing that loved ones will have a stable source of financial support.

4. Protection against Mismanagement: Trusts offer a layer of protection against mismanagement of assets by beneficiaries. The grantor can appoint a trustee who will oversee the management and distribution of the trust assets, ensuring that they are used for the intended purposes and in the best interests of the beneficiaries. This can help prevent the assets from being squandered or misused.

5. Special Needs Planning: Trusts are commonly used in special needs planning to provide financial security for individuals with disabilities. Special needs trusts can ensure that individuals with special needs receive the necessary support while preserving their eligibility for government benefits. These trusts can cover a wide range of expenses, including medical care, therapy, housing, transportation, and quality of life enhancements.

6. Minimization of Probate: Trusts can help bypass the probate process, which can be time-consuming, expensive, and public. By transferring assets to a trust, individuals can ensure a smooth and efficient transfer of wealth to their loved ones without the delays and costs associated with probate. This allows beneficiaries to access the assets more quickly and maintains privacy regarding the distribution of assets.

7. Multi-Generational Wealth Transfer: Trusts can be designed to preserve wealth and provide financial security for multiple generations. By establishing a dynasty trust, for example, individuals can transfer assets to future generations while minimizing estate taxes and preserving the assets' growth potential. This allows for the long-term financial security of descendants and the perpetuation of family wealth.

It's important to work with an experienced estate planning attorney to establish a trust that aligns with individual goals and circumstances. The attorney can provide guidance on trust structures, tax implications, and trustee selection to ensure that the trust effectively provides financial security for loved ones.

Overall, trust funds offer a powerful tool for providing financial security to loved ones. By utilizing trusts, individuals can protect assets, control distributions, provide ongoing support, and ensure that their loved ones are well taken care of in the future.

- Guide readers in utilizing trust funds for estate planning and seamless wealth transfer

Utilizing trust funds for estate planning and seamless wealth transfer requires careful consideration and understanding of the options available. Here is a step-by-step guide to help you navigate the process:

1. Identify Your Goals: Begin by clarifying your estate planning goals. Consider who you want to benefit from your assets, how you want those assets to be managed and distributed, and any specific needs or concerns you may have. This will help guide your decisions throughout the process.

2. Understand Trust Fund Options: Familiarize yourself with the different types of trust funds available. Common options include revocable living trusts, irrevocable trusts, testamentary trusts, special needs trusts, and charitable trusts. Each type has its own purpose and benefits, so it's essential to select the one that aligns with your goals and needs.

3. Engage Professionals: Seek the guidance of experienced professionals, such as an estate planning attorney and a financial advisor. They can assist you in understanding the legal and financial implications of trust funds, help you navigate the complex process, and ensure that your plan is legally sound and optimized for your specific circumstances.

4. Determine Trust Fund Structure: Work with your estate planning attorney to determine the appropriate structure for your trust fund. Consider factors such as the type of trust, the selection of trustees, successor trustees, and beneficiaries, as well as any specific instructions or conditions you want to include.

5. Fund the Trust: Transfer assets into the trust fund. This may involve changing the ownership of assets, such as real estate, bank accounts, investments, and other property, to the name of the trust.

Consult with your attorney to ensure that the transfer is done correctly and that all necessary legal requirements are met.

6. Designate Beneficiaries: Clearly identify and designate the beneficiaries of the trust. This can include individuals, organizations, or charities. Be specific about how you want the assets to be distributed and any conditions or restrictions you want to impose.

7. Appoint a Trustee: Select a trustee who will be responsible for managing the trust and carrying out your wishes. The trustee can be an individual, a professional trustee, or a corporate trustee, depending on your preferences and the complexity of the trust. It's important to choose someone who is trustworthy, capable, and aligned with your values.

8. Create a Plan for Succession: Plan for the succession of trustees in case the primary trustee is unable or unwilling to fulfill their duties. Designate successor trustees who can step in and continue managing the trust according to your wishes. This ensures a seamless transition and ongoing administration of the trust.

9. Review and Update Regularly: Estate planning is not a one-time event. Review and update your trust fund regularly to ensure it remains aligned with your evolving goals, family dynamics, and changes in the legal and financial landscape. Make adjustments as needed to reflect your current circumstances and preferences.

10. Communicate and Educate: Lastly, communicate your estate plan to your loved ones and beneficiaries. Ensure they understand your intentions, the role of the trust, and how it can benefit them. Providing education and guidance can help avoid misunderstandings or conflicts down the line.

Remember, estate planning and the use of trust funds can be complex, so it's crucial to work with professionals who can provide personalized advice and guidance. By following this guide and seeking professional assistance, you can effectively utilize trust funds for estate planning and ensure a seamless wealth transfer to your loved ones.

- Explore options for using trust funds to support education, healthcare, and other family needs

Trust funds can be an excellent tool for supporting education, healthcare, and other family needs. Here are some options to consider when utilizing trust funds for these purposes:

1. Education Trusts: Establishing an education trust can provide financial support for educational expenses, such as tuition fees, books, and living expenses. This type of trust can be set up specifically for a beneficiary's education or as a broader educational fund for multiple beneficiaries. The trust can be designed to provide regular distributions during the beneficiary's educational journey or as a lump sum payment upon reaching specific milestones.

2. Healthcare Trusts: Healthcare trusts can be created to cover medical expenses, health insurance premiums, and other healthcare-related costs for beneficiaries. These trusts are especially useful for individuals with specific healthcare needs or conditions. By setting up a healthcare trust, you can ensure that your loved ones have access to necessary medical care and support throughout their lives.

3. Special Needs Trusts: Special needs trusts are designed to provide financial support for individuals with disabilities or special needs. These trusts are structured in a way that allows beneficiaries to receive the necessary assistance without compromising their eligibility for government benefits. Special needs trusts can cover various expenses, including medical care, therapy, housing, transportation, and other quality-of-life enhancements.

4. Discretionary Trusts: A discretionary trust gives the trustee the discretion to distribute funds for various family needs as they arise. This type of trust allows the trustee to consider the specific circumstances and needs of each beneficiary and make distributions accordingly. Discretionary trusts can be flexible and adaptable, providing support for a wide range of family needs, including education, healthcare, housing, and other essential expenses.

5. Purpose-Specific Trusts: You can create purpose-specific trusts to address specific family needs. For example, you may establish a trust to support a family member's entrepreneurial ventures, artistic pursuits, or charitable endeavors. By tailoring the trust to a specific purpose, you can ensure that your loved ones have the financial resources to pursue their passions and goals.

6. Trust Protectors: Including trust protectors in the trust structure can add an extra layer of oversight and ensure that the trust funds are used for their intended purposes. Trust protectors can monitor the trust's administration, ensure compliance with the trust's provisions, and make decisions regarding distributions based on the defined purposes, such as education or healthcare.

7. Letter of Wishes: Alongside the trust, you can provide a letter of wishes to guide the trustee in making distribution decisions. This letter can outline your intentions, preferences, and instructions regarding how the trust funds should be used to support education, healthcare, and other family needs. While not legally binding, the letter can provide valuable guidance to the trustee.

When utilizing trust funds for education, healthcare, and other family needs, it's crucial to work closely with an experienced estate planning attorney. They can help you select the appropriate trust structure, draft the necessary legal documents, and ensure that your intentions are clearly stated and legally enforceable. Additionally, involving your family members in the planning process and discussing your intentions openly can help foster understanding and ensure that the trust funds are used in the best interests of your loved ones.

Chapter 8: Navigating Life Transitions: Adapting Trust Funds to Changing Circumstances

- Explain how trust funds can assist individuals during major life events like marriage, divorce, or retirement

Trust funds can play a significant role in supporting individuals during major life events such as marriage, divorce, or retirement. Here's how trust funds can assist individuals during these critical milestones:

1. Marriage:
- Pre-Nuptial Trusts: Trust funds can be used to establish pre-nuptial trusts, which can protect assets and provide financial security in the event of a divorce or separation. These trusts can help safeguard family wealth and ensure that assets are distributed according to predetermined terms in case the marriage ends.

- Spousal Support: Trust funds can be utilized to provide ongoing financial support to a spouse in the event of a divorce or separation. By setting up a trust, you can ensure that your spouse has access to a reliable source of income or other financial resources, helping to maintain their standard of living.

- Family Wealth Preservation: Trust funds can be structured to preserve family wealth and assets for future generations. By placing assets in a trust, you can protect them from potential claims or division during a divorce settlement and ensure that they remain within the family.

2. Divorce:
- Divorce Settlements: Trust funds can be used as part of a divorce settlement to provide financial support to the divorcing parties. This can include ongoing spousal support or the distribution of assets in a manner that meets the needs of both parties.

- Asset Protection: Establishing a trust before or during a marriage can help protect assets from being subject to division in the event of a divorce. By placing assets into a trust, they can be shielded from potential claims or division, allowing for greater control and protection of one's wealth.

- Child Support: Trust funds can also be utilized to ensure the continued financial support of children after a divorce. By setting up a trust, you can provide for the specific needs of your children, such as education, healthcare, and other expenses, while maintaining control over how the funds are used.

3. Retirement:
- Retirement Income: Trust funds can be designed to provide a reliable and consistent source of income during retirement. By establishing a retirement trust, you can ensure that you have sufficient funds to support your lifestyle and cover expenses throughout your retirement years.

- Healthcare and Long-Term Care: Trust funds can be used to plan for healthcare and long-term care expenses during retirement. By setting up a healthcare trust or long-term care trust, you can ensure that you have the necessary financial resources to cover medical costs and support your well-being as you age.

- Succession Planning: Trust funds can assist with succession planning, allowing for the smooth transfer of assets and wealth to the next generation. By establishing a trust, you can outline your wishes for the distribution of assets and provide for the financial needs of your beneficiaries during retirement and beyond.

It's important to work with an experienced estate planning attorney and financial advisor when utilizing trust funds during major life events like marriage, divorce, or retirement. They can help you understand the legal and financial implications, guide you in selecting the appropriate trust structure, and ensure that your intentions are effectively reflected in the trust's provisions.

- Discuss the flexibility of trust funds in adapting to changing circumstances and needs

Trust funds offer a high degree of flexibility in adapting to changing circumstances and needs. Here are some ways in which trust funds can be flexible:

1. Amendment and Modification: Trusts can often be amended or modified to accommodate changing circumstances and needs. If the original terms of the trust no longer align with your goals or the needs of the beneficiaries, you can work with an attorney to make necessary changes. This may involve adjusting distribution provisions, adding or removing beneficiaries, or changing the purpose of the trust.

2. Trustee Discretion: Many trusts grant the trustee discretion in making distributions and managing trust assets. This discretion allows the trustee to adapt to changing circumstances and needs of the beneficiaries. For example, if a beneficiary requires additional support due to unforeseen circumstances, the trustee can use their discretion to provide the necessary assistance, within the limits set by the trust.

3. Special Power of Appointment: Trusts can include a special power of appointment, which grants someone the authority to change the beneficiaries or the terms of the trust. This power can be used to respond to changes in family dynamics, such as the birth of new family members or the need to address changing financial circumstances.

4. Trust Protector: Some trusts include the role of a trust protector, who has the authority to modify certain aspects of the trust. The trust protector can exercise this power when specific conditions are met or when changes are needed to adapt to unforeseen circumstances. This provides an additional layer of flexibility in adjusting the trust to meet changing needs.

5. Trust Distribution Standards: Trusts can be structured with broad distribution standards that allow for flexibility in meeting the needs of beneficiaries. For example, a trust may specify that distributions can be made for the beneficiary's health, education, maintenance, or support. This allows the trustee to interpret and apply these standards in a way that responds to the beneficiary's evolving circumstances and needs.

6. Successor Trustees: Trusts can designate successor trustees who will take over the administration of the trust in the event that the initial trustee is unable or unwilling to continue. This ensures that there is a mechanism in place to manage the trust and make decisions in line with changing circumstances and needs.

7. Trust Termination: In certain situations, it may be possible to terminate a trust entirely if it no longer serves its intended purpose or if the circumstances warrant it. Termination may involve distributing the remaining assets to the beneficiaries or merging the trust with another trust to better meet the evolving needs of the beneficiaries.

It's important to note that the flexibility of trust funds may be subject to legal and tax considerations. It's advisable to work with an experienced estate planning attorney who can guide you through the process of modifying or adapting a trust to ensure compliance with applicable laws and regulations.

Overall, trust funds offer considerable flexibility in responding to changing circumstances and needs, allowing for adjustments to be made to align with the best interests of the beneficiaries and the intentions of the trust creator.

- Share inspiring stories of regular individuals who successfully navigated life transitions with the help of trust funds

Here are a few inspiring stories of regular individuals who successfully navigated life transitions with the help of trust funds:

1. Jane's Entrepreneurial Journey:
Jane had always dreamt of starting her own business but lacked the financial resources to do so. Fortunately, her parents had set up a trust fund for her education and future endeavors. With the support of the trust fund, Jane was able to pursue her entrepreneurial aspirations. The trust fund provided her with the initial capital she needed to launch her business and navigate the early stages of entrepreneurship. Today, Jane's business has flourished, and she attributes much of her success to the trust fund that provided her with the opportunity to pursue her passion.

2. Mark's Career Change:

Mark had been working in a high-paying but unfulfilling job for several years. He longed for a career change that aligned with his true passion for environmental conservation. However, the transition would require him to take a significant pay cut and invest in additional education and training. Luckily, Mark had a trust fund established by his grandparents. With the financial support from the trust fund, he was able to pursue the necessary education and training to make a successful career transition. Today, Mark is deeply satisfied with his work in environmental conservation and credits the trust fund for enabling him to follow his dreams.

3. Sarah's Family Support:

Sarah went through a challenging divorce that left her as the sole provider for her three young children. The divorce settlement included a trust fund for the children's support. The trust fund provided a stable source of financial assistance, ensuring that Sarah's children had their educational, healthcare, and everyday needs met. With the support of the trust fund, Sarah was able to focus on rebuilding her life and providing a secure future for her children. The trust fund acted as a safety net during a difficult time, allowing Sarah and her children to navigate the transition and build a brighter future.

4. John's Retirement Security:

John had worked diligently throughout his career and wisely invested in a retirement trust fund. As he approached retirement age, he realized that the trust fund would provide him with the financial security he needed to retire comfortably and pursue his passions. The trust fund ensured that John could maintain his desired lifestyle, travel, and indulge in hobbies during retirement. It offered him the peace of mind to embrace this new phase of life without financial worries, allowing him to fully enjoy the fruits of his labor.

These stories highlight the transformative impact that trust funds can have on individuals as they navigate various life transitions. Trust funds can provide the financial support and stability needed to pursue dreams, make career changes, overcome challenges, and enjoy a secure future. It's important to remember that each individual's circumstances and trust fund arrangements are unique, and consulting with legal and financial professionals is crucial for proper planning and execution.

Chapter 9: Leaving a Lasting Legacy: Charitable Trust Funds

- Highlight the power of trust funds in making a positive impact through philanthropy

Trust funds have the power to make a significant positive impact through philanthropy by providing a structured and sustainable approach to charitable giving. Here are some ways in which trust funds can contribute to philanthropic endeavors:

1. Long-Term Impact: Trust funds offer the advantage of long-term planning and sustainability. By establishing a trust fund for philanthropic purposes, individuals can ensure that their charitable giving continues beyond their lifetime. The funds can be invested and managed to generate income, which can then be used to support charitable causes for years to come. This allows for a lasting and meaningful impact on the communities and causes that matter most to the donor.

2. Focus and Strategy: Trust funds provide a framework for strategic giving. Donors can specify the purpose and focus of their philanthropy, whether it's supporting education, healthcare, the arts, environmental conservation, or any other cause close to their heart. Trust funds allow for the creation of clear guidelines and objectives, ensuring that charitable resources are directed toward specific goals and initiatives. This focused approach maximizes the impact of philanthropic efforts and helps address critical issues in a targeted manner.

3. Flexibility and Adaptability: Trust funds offer flexibility in adapting to changing needs and circumstances. Philanthropic goals and priorities may evolve over time, and trust funds can be structured to accommodate these changes. Donors can work with

trustees and advisors to modify the terms of the trust to align with emerging needs or emerging solutions. This ensures that charitable resources are effectively utilized and responsive to the ever-changing challenges faced by communities and society.

4. Professional Management: Trust funds provide access to professional investment and financial management expertise. Trustees, along with financial advisors, can help grow the assets of the trust fund through prudent investment strategies. This professional management ensures that the philanthropic resources are maximized and generate sustainable income to support charitable initiatives. Additionally, trustees can offer guidance and expertise in identifying impactful organizations and projects that align with the donor's philanthropic vision.

5. Donor Legacy: Trust funds allow donors to leave a lasting legacy. By establishing a trust fund for philanthropy, individuals can ensure that their values and commitment to making a difference are carried forward. Trust funds can be structured to involve future generations, allowing them to continue the family's tradition of giving and contributing to causes that are important to the family. This perpetuation of philanthropy creates a powerful legacy that can inspire others to engage in charitable acts and make a positive impact.

6. Tax Benefits: Trust funds can provide tax advantages for charitable giving. Depending on the jurisdiction, donations made through a trust fund may be eligible for tax deductions or other favorable tax treatment. This allows donors to optimize their philanthropic giving and potentially increase the resources available for charitable causes.

Overall, trust funds offer a robust and impactful mechanism for philanthropy. They provide the means to create a lasting positive impact, focus resources on specific causes, adapt to changing needs, leverage professional expertise, and leave a meaningful legacy. By harnessing the power of trust funds, individuals can make a significant difference in the lives of others and contribute to the betterment of society.

- Discuss the benefits of setting up charitable trust funds and incorporating charitable giving into financial planning

Setting up charitable trust funds and incorporating charitable giving into financial planning can offer several benefits. Let's explore some of them:

1. Fulfillment of Philanthropic Goals: Charitable trust funds provide a structured and dedicated avenue for individuals to fulfill their philanthropic goals. By establishing a trust fund, individuals can ensure that their charitable giving aligns with their values and priorities. It offers a systematic and intentional approach to make a positive impact on the causes and communities that matter most to them.

2. Tax Advantages: One of the key benefits of setting up charitable trust funds is the potential for tax advantages. Depending on the jurisdiction, contributions made to charitable trust funds may be tax-deductible. This can result in significant tax savings for donors and provide an opportunity to optimize their overall financial planning strategies.

3. Long-Term Sustainability: Charitable trust funds offer the advantage of long-term sustainability. By structuring the trust fund appropriately, individuals can ensure that their charitable giving continues beyond their lifetime. The trust assets can be invested and managed to generate income, which can then be used to support charitable causes indefinitely. This allows for a lasting and sustainable impact on the communities and causes being supported.

4. Estate Planning and Legacy: Incorporating charitable giving into financial planning through trust funds can play a crucial role in estate planning and creating a meaningful legacy. By setting up a charitable trust fund, individuals can specify how their assets will be distributed to charitable causes upon their death. This ensures that their philanthropic intentions are carried out and allows them to leave a lasting impact on the causes they care about. It also provides an opportunity to involve future generations in philanthropy, passing on the values of giving and making a difference.

5. Strategic and Impactful Giving: Incorporating charitable giving into financial planning through trust funds allows for strategic and impactful giving. Donors can define the purpose and focus of their philanthropy, ensuring that their resources are directed towards causes that align with their values and have a significant impact. By working with trustees, financial advisors, and philanthropic experts, donors can develop effective strategies to maximize the impact of their charitable giving.

6. Personal and Family Values: Charitable trust funds provide a platform for individuals and families to express and uphold their personal and family values. It allows them to support causes that are meaningful to them and make a difference in areas they are passionate about. By incorporating charitable giving into financial planning, individuals can integrate their values into their overall wealth management strategy, creating a sense of purpose and fulfillment.

7. Recognition and Influence: Charitable trust funds can provide opportunities for recognition and influence in the philanthropic community. By establishing a trust fund and actively engaging in charitable giving, individuals can become part of a network of like-minded donors and organizations. This can lead to collaborations, partnerships, and increased visibility for the causes they support, amplifying their impact and influence.

Incorporating charitable trust funds and charitable giving into financial planning offers a holistic and purpose-driven approach to wealth management. It allows individuals to align their financial resources with their philanthropic goals, optimize tax benefits, create a lasting legacy, and make a meaningful impact on the causes they care about. It's important to consult with legal, financial, and philanthropic professionals to ensure that the trust fund is structured appropriately and aligns with the donor's objectives.

- Provide guidance on how regular individuals can leave a lasting legacy through charitable trust funds

Leaving a lasting legacy through charitable trust funds is a meaningful way for regular individuals to make a lasting impact on the causes they care about. Here is some guidance on how to achieve this:

1. Identify Your Passion and Values: Start by identifying the causes and issues that are most important to you. Reflect on your values, personal experiences, and the issues that resonate with you. Consider areas such as education, healthcare, the environment, social justice, or any other cause that aligns with your passion and values.

2. Determine Your Philanthropic Goals: Clarify your philanthropic goals and objectives. What specific outcomes do you want to achieve? Do you want to support a particular organization, fund scholarships, or address a specific social issue? Defining your goals will help guide your decision-making process when setting up your charitable trust fund.

3. Research and Seek Professional Advice: Conduct thorough research on charitable trust funds and seek professional advice from legal, financial, and philanthropic experts. They can provide guidance on the legal and financial aspects of setting up a trust fund, help you understand the tax implications, and offer insights into effective philanthropic strategies.

4. Choose the Right Trust Structure: Work with professionals to determine the most suitable trust structure for your philanthropic goals. Common options include donor-advised funds, private foundations, or supporting organizations. Each structure has its own benefits and considerations, so it's important to understand the differences and select the one that aligns with your objectives.

5. Select Trusted Trustees: Choose trustees who will oversee the administration and management of your charitable trust fund. Trustees should be individuals or organizations that share your values and have the necessary expertise to effectively manage the fund. They will be responsible for making grant decisions and ensuring that the fund's resources are used in accordance with your philanthropic goals.

6. Define Grantmaking Guidelines: Establish clear guidelines and criteria for awarding grants from your trust fund. Determine the types of organizations or projects that are eligible for funding, the geographic focus, and the impact areas you want to support. Clear guidelines will help ensure that your charitable giving stays aligned with your objectives and values.

7. Involve Loved Ones and Future Generations: Consider involving your loved ones and future generations in your philanthropic journey. You can engage them by including them as trustees, creating a family giving plan, or establishing a donor-advised fund that allows them to participate in grantmaking decisions. Involving family members can help create a lasting legacy and instill a sense of philanthropy in future generations.

8. Continuously Evaluate and Adapt: Regularly evaluate the impact of your charitable trust fund and make adjustments as needed. Stay informed about the causes you support, monitor the performance of your trust fund's investments, and assess the effectiveness of the organizations you fund. By continuously evaluating and adapting, you can ensure that your trust fund remains impactful and aligned with your philanthropic goals over time.

9. Communicate Your Legacy Intentions: Communicate your philanthropic intentions and legacy plans to your loved ones, trustees, and the organizations you support. This will help ensure that your wishes are known and understood, and it can provide inspiration for others to get involved in charitable giving.

Remember, leaving a lasting legacy through a charitable trust fund requires thoughtful planning, ongoing engagement, and collaboration with professionals. By following these steps, regular individuals can create a legacy that positively impacts the causes they are passionate about and creates a better future for generations to come.

Conclusion:

- Recap the key benefits and advantages of trust funds for regular individuals

Here is a recap of the key benefits and advantages of trust funds for regular individuals:

1. Fulfillment of Philanthropic Goals: Trust funds provide a structured and dedicated avenue for individuals to fulfill their philanthropic goals and make a positive impact on the causes and communities they care about.

2. Tax Advantages: Depending on the jurisdiction, contributions made to trust funds may be tax-deductible, resulting in potential tax savings for donors and optimizing their overall financial planning strategies.

3. Long-Term Sustainability: Trust funds offer the advantage of long-term sustainability. By investing and managing the trust assets, individuals can ensure that their charitable giving continues beyond their lifetime, creating a lasting and sustainable impact.

4. Estate Planning and Legacy: Trust funds play a crucial role in estate planning and creating a meaningful legacy. Individuals can specify how their assets will be distributed to charitable causes upon their death, ensuring that their philanthropic intentions are carried out and leaving a lasting impact.

5. Strategic and Impactful Giving: Trust funds allow for strategic and impactful giving. Donors can define the purpose and focus of their philanthropy, ensuring that their resources are directed towards causes that align with their values and have a significant impact.

6. Personal and Family Values: Trust funds provide a platform for individuals and families to express and uphold their personal and family values. They allow for support of causes that are meaningful, integrating values into overall wealth management strategies.

7. Recognition and Influence: Trust funds can provide opportunities for recognition and influence in the philanthropic community. By actively engaging in charitable giving, individuals can become part

of a network of like-minded donors and organizations, amplifying their impact and influence.

Incorporating trust funds into financial planning offers a holistic and purpose-driven approach to wealth management. They allow individuals to align their financial resources with their philanthropic goals, optimize tax benefits, create a lasting legacy, and make a meaningful impact on the causes they care about. It's important to consult with professionals to ensure the trust fund is structured appropriately and aligns with the donor's objectives.

- Emphasize the importance of seeking professional guidance in establishing and managing trust funds

Seeking professional guidance is crucial when it comes to establishing and managing trust funds. Here's why:

1. Expertise and Knowledge: Professionals in the legal, financial, and philanthropic fields have the expertise and knowledge to guide you through the complexities of trust fund establishment and management. They understand the legal requirements, tax implications, and best practices, ensuring that your trust is structured appropriately and in compliance with regulations.

2. Tailored Advice: Every individual's financial situation and goals are unique. Professionals can provide personalized advice based on your specific circumstances, helping you choose the most suitable type of trust, determine the optimal funding strategy, and align the trust's objectives with your values and aspirations.

3. Maximizing Benefits: Trust fund professionals can help you maximize the benefits of establishing a trust. They can advise you on tax planning strategies, explore opportunities for asset protection, and ensure that your trust is designed to meet your long-term financial goals.

4. Compliance and Risk Mitigation: Trusts are subject to various legal and regulatory requirements. Professionals can ensure that your trust is structured and managed in compliance with these rules, minimizing the risk of legal issues or challenges in the future.

5. Investment Management: Trust funds often involve investment of assets to generate returns. Professionals can provide guidance on investment strategies, asset allocation, and risk management, helping you optimize the performance of the trust's assets and achieve your financial objectives.

6. Ongoing Administration and Reporting: Trust funds require ongoing administration and reporting. Professionals can handle these tasks, ensuring that the trust is properly administered, tax filings are completed accurately and on time, and beneficiaries receive the necessary information and support.

7. Peace of Mind: Seeking professional guidance provides peace of mind. Knowing that you have professionals overseeing the establishment and management of your trust fund gives you confidence that it is being handled competently and in your best interests.

Establishing and managing a trust fund is a complex process that requires careful consideration and expertise. By working with professionals, you can navigate the intricacies of trust law, optimize your financial planning, and ensure that your trust fund aligns with your goals and values. Don't hesitate to reach out to legal, financial, and philanthropic professionals who specialize in trust funds to guide you on your journey. Their knowledge and experience will be invaluable in helping you achieve your financial objectives and create a secure future.

- Encourage readers to take action and embark on their trust fund journey to achieve financial success and a secure future

I encourage you to take action and embark on your trust fund journey to achieve financial success and create a secure future. Here's why:

1. Financial Security: Trust funds provide a reliable and structured way to secure your financial future. By setting aside funds in a trust, you can protect and grow your assets, ensuring financial stability for yourself and your loved ones.

2. Wealth Preservation: Trust funds offer a powerful tool for preserving wealth across generations. By establishing a trust, you can strategically manage and protect your assets, minimizing tax liabilities and ensuring that your wealth is passed on to future generations in accordance with your wishes.

3. Tax Planning: Trust funds provide opportunities for tax planning and optimization. Depending on the structure of the trust and the jurisdiction, you may be able to take advantage of tax benefits and deductions, reducing your overall tax burden and maximizing your wealth accumulation.

4. Legacy Building: Trust funds enable you to leave a lasting legacy. By setting up a trust, you can ensure that your assets are used to support causes and organizations that are important to you, leaving a positive impact on society and creating a meaningful legacy.

5. Philanthropic Fulfillment: Trust funds offer a pathway to fulfill your philanthropic aspirations. By incorporating charitable giving into your trust structure, you can support causes and make a difference in areas that are close to your heart, bringing fulfillment and purpose to your financial journey.

6. Professional Guidance: Setting up a trust fund may seem complex, but professionals in the legal, financial, and philanthropic fields can guide you through the process. They can help you understand the options available, navigate the legal and financial considerations, and design a trust that aligns with your goals and values.

7. Empowerment and Control: Trust funds provide a sense of empowerment and control over your financial future. By proactively managing your assets through a trust, you can have a greater say in how your wealth is utilized, ensuring that it aligns with your values and goals.

8. Peace of Mind: Knowing that you have a well-structured trust fund in place can bring peace of mind. It provides a sense of security, knowing that you have taken steps to protect and grow your

wealth, support your loved ones, and make a positive impact on the causes you care about.

Embarking on a trust fund journey requires careful planning, professional guidance, and a commitment to your financial goals. I encourage you to take action today, explore the options available, and start building a secure financial future while making a meaningful impact. Your trust fund journey can be a transformative experience that sets you on a path to financial success and leaves a lasting legacy.

Note: This detailed outline aims to provide a comprehensive guide for regular individuals interested in setting up and leveraging trust funds. It covers the essential aspects of trust funds, including setup, asset protection, tax advantages, family security, life transitions, and charitable giving. The outline provides a step-by-step approach, practical tips, and real-life examples to make the information accessible and actionable for readers.

Dear Reader's,

I wanted to take a moment to express my heartfelt gratitude for your engagement and interest in my book on trust funds. Your dedication to expanding your knowledge in this area is truly commendable, and I hope that the information I provided has been helpful in your understanding of trust funds.

As an author, my ultimate goal is to provide valuable and insightful content that resonates with readers like yourself. Your support and feedback are incredibly important to me, as they help me improve my work and reach a wider audience.

I would be immensely grateful if you could take a few moments to leave an honest review of my book. Your review will not only help me understand what you found valuable or enjoyable about the book, but it will also guide other potential readers in making an informed decision. Your thoughts and experiences are valuable, and I believe they can make a real difference in the lives of others who are seeking guidance in this area.

I understand that leaving a review may take a little time and effort, but please know that your contribution will have a lasting impact. Your honest feedback will not only help me grow as an author but also assist others in making informed choices when it comes to trust funds.

Thank you once again for your support and for considering leaving a review. I truly appreciate your time and input.

Warmest regards,
M Livingston